T0246861

Moling in Meditation

Moling in Meditation
A Psalter for an Early Irish Monk

PAUL MURRAY O.P.

St. Augustine's Press
South Bend, Indiana

Manufactured in the United States of America.

1 2 3 4 5 6   28 27 26 25 24 23

**Library of Congress Control Number:
2023930177**

Hardback ISBN: 978-1-58731-519-0
ebook ISBN: 978-1-59831-520-6

∞ The paper used in this publication meets the minimum
requirements of the American National Standard for
Information Sciences –
Permanence of Paper for Printed Materials, ANSI Z39.48-
1984.

St. Augustine's Press
www.staugustine.net

To
Ben and Tina

Contents

Introduction

Moling, a man, a monk, a saint of the seventh-century, comes towards us out of history wrapped in wonder and myth. He is, in the Irish literary and spiritual tradition, the figure, I would say, who most resembles St Francis of Assisi. The bond, we are told, existing between him and nature, both wild and tame, was one of intimacy and joy. According to Douglas Hyde in *The Literary History of Ireland,* the life of Moling 'seems to have taken peculiar hold upon the imagination of the populace,'[1] an enchantment which continued long after his death. In later centuries poets had no hesitation or scruple in ascribing poems of their own to the Irish monk. Hyde writes: 'Moling has more poems … attributed to him than we find ascribed to any of the saints except Columcille.'[2] Mindful of that tradition – and though a decidedly modest part of it – I have made bold, in the sequence which follows, to ascribe all the newly composed lyrics, forty two in number, to

1 Douglas Hyde, *A Literary History of Ireland: From Earliest Times to the Present Day* (New York 1901; reprinted London 2016) p.210.
2 Ibid.

Moling.[3] Some are directly inspired by traditional legends, but none are based on any of the surviving fragments composed by Moling himself.[4]

According to hagiographical tradition St Moling enjoyed close and happy relations with all kinds of animals, among them a wren, a tiny fly, and a fox. The fly, we're told, made music for him, buzzing in his ear 'when he came back from Matins.'[5] And the fox, though wild, had no hesitation in eating 'out of his hand.'[6] One of the lyrics

---

3 A small number of these lyrics appeared first in an earlier book of poems, *The Absent Fountain* (Dedalus Press, Dublin 1991).

4 See 'Poems ascribed to S. Moling,' transcribed by Whitely Stokes, in *Anecdota from Irish Manuscripts,* Vol II, edited by O.J. Bergin, R.I. Best, Kuno Meyer, J.G. O'Keeffe (Dublin 1908) pp.20–41.

5 These arresting details come from an early Gaelic manuscript edited and translated by Whitely Stokes. See *The Birth and Life of Moling*, 73. (Dublin 2021) p.51. This work appeared originally in a 1907 edition published by Stokes in London entitled *Specimens of Middle-Irish Literature, No. 1, Geinemain Molling ocus a Bhetae.*

6 For this detail see *'Vita sancti Moling,'* in *Vitae Sanctorum Hiberniae,* Vol. 2, ed., Charles Plummer (Oxford 1910) p.201. The full story of the monk and the fox, as it appeared in the ancient *Vita,* was translated by Helen Waddell. See 'St Moling and the Fox,' *Beasts and Saints* (London 1995; first published 1934) pp.96–97.

included in the present sequence is entitled 'Address to Brother Fox'. It might seem, given the title, that I am borrowing or stealing the appellation from Francis of Assisi. But the phrase 'Brother Fox' made its first appearance, as it happens, in early Irish monastic literature.[7] 'The Irish,' according to the English scholar Robin Flower, 'were naturally Franciscan, Franciscan before St Francis. For when we read the records of the early [Irish] Church, the legends, the poems, the rules … these records have that very air of morning freshness which surrounds the early Franciscan traditions.'[8] So impressed, on one occasion, was the poet Seamus Heaney by the surviving lyrics of the early Irish monks, he remarked that a major part of their achievement was in making 'a springwater music out of certain feelings in a way unmatched in any other European language.'[9] And he noted further: 'We are nearer the first world in that first poetry, nearer to the innocent

7 See 'Vita Sancti Ciarani de Saigir,' in Vitae Sanctorum Hiberniae, Vol.1, pp. 219–220. The fox, referred to in this particular story as 'Brother Fox,' had stolen the shoes of the abbot. He eventually brought them back uneaten and was forgiven by the saint.

8 Robin Flower, The Irish Tradition (Oxford 1978, first published 1947) p.125.

9 Seamus Heaney, 'The God in the Tree: Early Irish Nature Poetry,' in Preoccupations: Selected Prose 1968–1978 (London 1980) p.182.

eye and tongue of Adam as he named the crea-
tures.'[10]

Information about the life of Moling can be
found in quite a number of early Irish manuscripts,
and what emerges from these sources is the figure of
a monk who belongs at least as much to legend as to
history. Moling, it's said, was born in 614, the ille-
gitimate son of a wealthy landowner called Fáelán
the Fair. At an early age he became a monk at
Glendalough in the Wicklow mountains.
Subsequently, he became responsible for the build-
ing of a number of churches, most notably the
church and monastery of St Mullin's in County
Carlow. It is there, according to the sources, that he
died in 696.[11] Clearly, Moling represented many
things to many people both during his life and after
his death. His most important biographer does not
hesitate to celebrate the quite extraordinary range of
his achievement, naming him as 'a poet, a knower,
a teacher, a sage, a psalmist, a priest, a bishop, a
soulfriend, a noble.'[12]

[10] Ibid.
[11] The *Latin* version of the *Life,* when speaking of
Moling's death, employs a rather striking and original
phrase: 'The holy priest Moling migrated most happily
to Christ.' See Máire B. de Paor, *Saint Moling Luachra*
(Dublin 2001) p.14.
[12] See *The Birth and Life of Moling*, 76, (Dublin 2021)
p.57.

The stories about Moling contain not only wisdom but also, on occasion, some measure of good humor, and that's no surprise. Robin Flower, reflecting on the work of many of the early Irish authors, refers to 'that ironic humor which goes hand in hand with the simplicity and clear mysticism of their legends.'[13] One story worth recounting describes an encounter between Moling and the Devil.

Once when Moling was at prayer in the church, he saw a young man coming towards him, handsome and well dressed.

'Hail, cleric!' the Devil says.

'Hail to you,' Moling replies.

Since Moling does not at once offer a blessing, which would have been customary, the Devil asks for an explanation. Moling, suspicious of the stranger, asks:

'Who are you?'.

'I am Christ, Son of God,' the Devil declares.

'I'm not at all sure about that,' replies Moling. 'When Christ would come to talk to the servants of God it was not in purple or with royal pomp he would come but in the form of a poor, hapless man, a leper.'

'So, you don't believe me?' the Devil says. 'Who, then, do you think I am?'

13 Robin Flower, *The Irish Tradition*, p.66.

'I think you are the Devil come to do me harm.'

'That unbelief,' the Devil replies, 'will bring ill for you.'

'What brought you here?', Moling asks.

'That you may bestow your blessing upon me,' replies the Devil.

'I will not bestow it,' exclaims Moling, 'for you don't deserve it.'

'Well then,' the Devil says, 'bestow the full of a curse on me.'

'But what good would that do you?' asks Moling.

'Easy to answer, O cleric! The curse will leave its venom and its hurt on your lips even as you speak it.'

'Be off with you!' declares Moling, 'you don't merit a blessing.'

'But, tell me, how could I merit it?' asks the Devil.

'By serving God,' says Moling.

'Alas,' the Devil replies, 'that I can't do.'

'Study then?'

'No, nor study, it's just as hopeless.'

'Fasting then?' says Moling.

'I've been fasting since the beginning of the world and I'm not one whit the better for it.'

'Making genuflections?'

'I cannot bend forward for backwards are my knees.'

'Be off with you then,' declares Moling, 'for I can neither teach you nor help you.'[14]

Moling's most memorable appearance in literature is not, as it happens, in one of his own poems, but in the medieval Irish work *Buile Suibhne,* the celebrated story of Mad Sweeney, a king from the north of Ireland who, as a result of being cursed, was changed into a bird and condemned to live out his days as an excommunicate in the wild. Flitting from one place to another, Sweeney appears as a wounded misfit – an image of the artist, Seamus Heaney calls him, 'displaced, guilty, assuaging himself by his utterance.'[15] Condemned to undergo the most extreme form of exile, he finds himself exploring

---

14 The story of Moling's encounter with the Devil can be found in 'The Martyrology of Oengus the Culdee,' a section of an Irish medieval work entitled *The Book of Leinster.* 'The Martyrology' was translated and published privately by Whitely Stokes in London, 1905. The extract cited here, 'St Moling and the Devil,' represents a slightly changed and abbreviated version of the Stokes translation.

15 Seamus Heaney, 'Introduction' in *Sweeney Astray: A Version from the Irish* (London 1983) p.ii. The reflections on the poetry of Sweeney in the paragraphs which follow appeared in a somewhat different form in my book, *God's Spies: Michelangelo, Shakespeare, and Other Poets of Vision* (Bloomsbury 2019) pp.165–66.

states of thought and feeling far outside the ordinary
spectrum. His language, as a result, his music, is one
with no protective covering, a poetry, in Heaney's
phrase, 'piercingly exposed to the beauties and
severities of the natural world.'[16]

> Never to hear a human voice!
> To sleep naked every night
> up there in the highest thickets.
>
> To have lost my proper shape and looks,
> a mad scuttler on mountain peaks,
> a derelict doomed to loneliness.[17]

Fortunately, the story does not end there. When,
by a kind providence, the exiled poet finally meets
Moling, he finds in the monk not only a great wel-
come but also a deep and compassionate under-
standing. They enjoy long conversations together,
and Moling takes care to see that Sweeney is prop-
erly fed and looked after. On one occasion, address-
ing the hungry Bird Man, Moling says: 'Come here
and share / whatever morsels you would like.'[18] To
this Sweeney replies 'There are worse things, priest,
than hunger. / Imagine living without a cloak.'

16 Ibid.
17 *Sweeney Astray,* 61, p.68.
18 Ibid., 75, p.77.

Stunned by these words, Moling exclaims: 'Then you are welcome to my smock, / and welcome to take my cowl.'[19]

Official religion, at the beginning of Sweeney's story, had been poorly represented. But here, at the end, Sweeney finds in Moling a man, a priest, who is genuinely kind and attentive. That said, however, in the eyes of Moling, Sweeney is no mere object of charity. Right from the beginning he recognizes in the crazed visionary something which commands complete respect. Sweeney, for his part, is aware that, in meeting Moling, he is encountering a man who has knowledge of the Gospel – living knowledge – and he is happy to acknowledge that authority. 'You are,' he declares to Moling, 'gifted with the Word.'[20]

While Sweeney has no hesitation in showing respect for Moling, at the same time he never forgets that, as a poet, he is in possession of another kind of knowledge, one which has its own truth. Accordingly, with a poet's natural pride, he declares, 'The Lord makes me his oracle / from

19 Ibid., 75, p.78.
20 Ibid., 75, p.77. The reconciliation witnessed at the end of *Buile Suibhne* between Sweeney and Moling, though genuine and, at times, deeply moving, cannot be said to represent a complete reconciliation. Seamus Heaney, in his introduction to *Sweeney Astray*, speaks of 'the closing pages of uneasy reconciliation.'

sunrise till sun's going down.'[21] To these words Moling answers with an immediately affirming statement, happy and willing to acknowledge the poet's unique authority: 'Then speak to us of hidden things, / give us tidings of the Lord.'[22]

The poems and meditations in the sequence which follows are voiced for Moling but none of them, it goes without saying, will add to our knowledge of the actual man and saint. I am writing here in the margins of a great tradition, by no means unaware of the risks and limitations involved in such an undertaking. Is it a wise or a foolish undertaking? Will certain ideas and images in the poems not inevitably betray a modern rather than a medieval sensibility? The only honest answer to this question is, of course, yes. But my hope, my prayer, is that any intrusions of mine from 'the margins,' as it were, will be treated with kindness and understanding by my readers. In the end what matters is that, in one form or another, a tribute in verse is being offered to a world of life and spirit from which we, as moderns, have still so much to learn.

21 Ibid.
22 Ibid.

A Note on the Illustrations

All the illustrations inside the book are reproduced from images which accompanied the text of a celebrated collection of Gaelic folk lore entitled Carmina Gadelica: Hymns and Incantations. This work was edited and published by Alexander Carmichael at Edinburgh in 1900. Mary Frances Carmichael, the wife of the editor, adapted the illustrations from early medieval insular manuscripts and engraved stones. From these illustrations I have chosen five to introduce the five sections of the Moling sequence: Fox, Serpent, Fire, Bird, and Scroll.

1
FOX

Vocation

I was young when I first came
to the monastery.
                For hours
I would stand outside the gate
and watch the monks at work
and prayer, grey cowls over
their heads, black sandals
on their feet.
                What struck me
forcibly was the silence
of the air around them. To me
it seemed they moved
and breathed in another world,
as if under water.

But how to explain the huge
impact of that silence?
                It entered
my chest like a wide river.
I had no time
to think or choose,
                my mind
caught like a tiny leaf

or feather,
                    unable to resist
the call,
yet happy and unafraid
to be drawn
into the strong current.

On Praying the Psalms

Because of the Divine Indwelling,
and for no other reason,
when a monk holds in his hands
the book of psalms
and begins to pray,
even his most simple thoughts
and words
give tongue, give breath
to the breathing of God.

Three Things I Love

1
Mist
The promise of warmth
when the dawn mist, that wide
shimmering cloud, is gone,
its white arms no longer clinging
to the tops of trees
or to the dark corners of the valley.

2
Smoke
The promise of warmth
when, at the open hearth
at dusk,
the dark smoke first begins to rise
from the crackling wood.

3
Spray
The promise of warmth
when, on the bleak ocean at dawn,
fresh winds from the south

blow against the incoming tides,
and the cold lifting spray
is lit by the sun.

Thoughts after Meditation

How these things happen
it is hard to say,
how, over time, I turned
interpreter of leaf-fall
and star-fall,
                    my mind
held in thrall
not only by the things
of highest heaven
                    but also
by the things of earth,
things as plain and simple
to the eye
as they are amazing.

Haze

Midday. The sun lies heavy
on my hands and arms.
In the trees, in the branches
hanging above my head,
the birds are quiet.
A wave of heat has settled
over the land, haze
on the lakes of still water.

Confession of a Sober Monk

After drinking in for years
the new wine of your Word
I should be sodden-drunk, reeling
like a holy fool,
        tipsy
with gratitude and praise.
But, far from attaining
that mad, that unhinged state
of joy, I have remained
        a slave
to norms and forms, a dullard
of the spirit. Sensible. *Sane*.

Address to Brother Fox

You are without fear.
You take the scraps of meat
from my hands.
You even curl up here
beside me on the grass.
But I am not fooled.
Both of us know the score:
you are as bold and sly
a thief as any in the world.

Can a monk be fond of a thief?

Well, there is a thief
of whom – let me declare it –
I am more fond
than anyone of earth or heaven,
and that's my Lord and God.
It's hard to credit,
but he's more cunning, more truly
deadly at this game
than you, my Brother Fox.

You would rob me of my shoes,

but his great aim
is to rob me of the things
that hold me still in bondage.
Thus, the false idols
to which I cling
he pounces on like prey, the bright
sharp spear of his love
tunnelling and burrowing.

With you, how often I'm reminded
of my Saviour!

His colour, like yours, is red,
red like a leaf in autumn,
red like a dying sun,
red like the blush of a virgin,
red like martyr's blood,
red like the arc of a rainbow,
red like a poppy field,
red like the bells of the fuchsia,
named for the tears of God.

How can I not be fond of you,
Brother Fox?
Even now, as I watch you
disappear in a rush of colour,
you remind me

of my wondrous, hidden Lord:
his swift beauty, like yours,
now here, now gone –
a red flame on the hill.

2
SERPENT

A Warning

Begin as you wish
and pursue
your own line of thought
or feeling
but be prepared
to be surprised.

Sometimes
within the first word
of a sentence,
or in the first letter
of a word,
are loops and turns.

And almost every scribe
or learned copyist
has seen
    – emerging
from the green
innocence of a tree –

the most lovely
curve of thought

or arc
of feeling
slowly uncoil itself
into a serpent.

Siren

That treacherous
              song,
that siren music
which, for days on end,
its magic
        coursing through
my blood,
        had aimed
to hold me in thrall,
is now ending,
              and with
infinitesimal sound,
as if the mouth
        of a tulip
closed, the bright
wings folded.

Love and Hate

Love grows in the cracks
between happiness.

Hate crawls to the stem
and to the blossom.

A Question to the Bird Man

For years your only friend
was pain,
the only word on your lips was
Why?
How did you survive?

I clung to hope.
I waited.
I tasted on my tongue,
like tears,
the timeless bitter words
for hurt and loss.

And then I swallowed
one by one
their grieving syllables.

The Lesson

More head than heart
more pride than sense,
I tried to sift
God's word like wheat,
I hungered
for absolute corn.
It was a pointless task –

Since, with the vain
and with the vulgar,
God has shared his bread
and, through his poets
and his saints, has said:
'To me
nothing human is alien.'

The Pursuit

Not with a calm purpose,
like a god, but with a lost
and urgent passion
you now pursue me, Lord,
even into my dreams,
sighing and asking: 'Do you
love me more than these?'

The Dark Thought

Who or what whispered: *Carry it
to prayer*? This thing of evil,
more like a stone lodged in my heart
than a dark thought, a thing
so hard to bear and so heavy
it weighed me down for days.

How, then, explain what happened?
How interpret this thing of wonder –
that almost in a second, and
with miraculous ease, the weight
grew light like flesh in water
and the burden of days was lifted?

Brief Confession

How confused I had been
from the start, how crazed!
A slave, now to fear, now
to pride, for years I fought
the carnal logic of my senses
until my mind was passionate
and my passions cold.
What a surprise, what a blessing
to discover that the realms
of time and eternity, flesh
and spirit, darkness
and light, are not enemies
but, given the freedom of
grace, more like siblings, more
like sisters and brothers.

After Reading Psalm 42

Is there a sadness
greater
than never to know
desire for God
as fierce and true as the
deer's thirst
for the chill earth-tasting
springs
of heath and hill?

Lightning

In the fissure of the moment
in the sudden lightning
of God's mercy

the saint
is indistinguishable
from the sinner

and the flowers of earth
and the flowers of heaven
are the same.

3
FIRE

Ego Scriptor

Steep
is the path before me
and dark the issue.
The time for mere words
is over.

Yet here am I
still trying
to compose
in this bright margin
one lean poem.

The Serene Dead

Maybe there is only a strip
of shadow between their world
and ours? Maybe they are
as near to us now as the tall
handsome ferns in the garden
or as the sounding river
or as the light in the darkening sky
or as the balm of jasmine
in the air, or as those lifting
sparks, the tiny fires of
glow worms glimpsed, half-glimpsed
in the bonfire-smoky dusk?

O God my God

You have slain me
with the sword of quiet

and in my blood again
that stillness

as if the throb of life itself
had paused.

Who are You?

You have stolen my faith.
You have taken the breath
from my mouth.

I wanted to pray,
I wanted to name your name.
I wanted to use again
the great, the hallowed words.

But you have frozen my tongue,
you have stolen my thoughts
and my words.
You have played a thieving game.

Who are you?

The Struggle

1

Some nights I feel like Jacob
fighting with an angel, and I'm
almost afraid to win.

2

Why must the soul
wrestle for its own relief?

My mind
interrogates me –

its questions like small
devils trying to catch me

by the throat.

Miracle

After days of drought
the honeyed music of rain
splashing down

out of the heavens.
The air so fresh now,
so cleansed, it feels

almost as if the throats
of the dead
can begin to breathe.

A Strange Mercy

Nothing prepared me for this.
Although I'd known for years that
fire,
according to the prophets, stands
for the nature of God,
I'd known it only in my head
and from the vellum of books.

So, when He seized hold of me,
I was startled,
first by the humbling, purifying flame
I felt in that embrace,
the stark illumination, the dawning shame
of self uncovered.

But then, lit by that first fire
of a strange mercy,
there came a second fire, impossible to

name or to explain,
a fire now all-consuming, an intimacy,
a wound of joy.

4
BIRD

Out in the Open

What new world is this?
I look up
and curls of light in the clouds are parables
of meaning.

I walk out into the garden
and the strewn perfumes of gorse
and wild orchid
are a summoning fragrance.

I walk down towards
the forest
and all around are covenants
gleaming
on flora and foliage,
on thorn bush and bracken.

What radiance – what bright madness is this?

The Happiness of Moling

Contented in both quiet
and disquiet, I was
a saint without a halo,

shattered and yet happy,
winning
on a losing hand,

saving my own
and others' lives
daily and hourly.

Force-fed by need,
fulfilled
by hunger,

I became
a beggar among beggars,
a foolish god

dependent on that love
which feeds
on its own bestowal,

asking for no gifts
and yet
receiving them hourly,

learning, first,
not to expect
too much

and, later,
not to expect
anything at all.

Today

A dread apocalypse, we thought,
hung over us –
what fists of hail, what storms,
what blasts of air!
It was as if loud trumpets
sounded
from the very throat of hell.

Our hope, it seemed, had drowned
in the flooding dark.
But now, hours later, all is still,
not one cloud in the sky.
We look up.
The rising moon
rinses our eyes with silver.

The Bird Man

1

Pity the mad poet.
Never!
He will despise your pity.

Rather envy him his madness.

He who has climbed
like a stray thrush
far into the sky, and has brushed

with his wings the stark
perils
of inner and outer storms,

the white pain,
arrows of white stars,
forked lightning.

2

Pity the mad poet.
Never!

A nomad, a drifter,
his soul is like that of a god
scattered and broken

and yet his vision
holds steady and clear,
his thoughts,

rain-washed and pebble-cold,
his words,
bright spears of frost.

3

Pity the mad poet,
Never!
He will despise your pity.

Although atremble
with fear and cold, asway
on the topmost

branches, often at night
he can hear,
coursing through his blood,

the music

of the tilting world.
He is alive,

although with broken
purpose and with wounded
nerves, he is alive.

4
Pity the mad poet.
Never!

Though he remains
an outcast, lost and feathered,
uniquely from his lips

there fall anointed words.
And, though old wounds,
old hurts,

still glitter in his dreams,
and daily torment
is his fate,

at times he lifts his gaze
and is the celebrant
of things

both luminous
and ordinary,
a psalmist of the cold light

after rain,
and of the last gleams
of light

between dusk and dark.

Winter

No season of the year more
stark, more beautiful:
frost, as far as the eye can see,
whitening the scrawny tufts
of grass and the bleak
low-lying forest boughs,
its cold hand fingering
the leaf-tips of aspen and holly,
of foxglove and fern.

Such things as these awaken
my now aged eyes to the strong
fierce beauty of my Lord.

At Dawn

Listen –
there it is again,
a linnet

undaunted by the storm,
its song
narrowing the gap

between
my mind not yet
fully awake

and the undimmed,
rain-washed
miracle of things.

On Perseverance

Should there come a day
when the dust of tedium settles
on your book of psalms,
and your repeated prayer seems never
to reach its mark,
tell yourself not to lose heart
or lose patience.
Walk down to the edge of the tide
and reflect there
on the patience of earth,
how the bright, cold waves
never tire of flowing in upon the dry,
welcoming sand.

Scandal in the Forest

A friend of mine
for years,
one of my closest neighbours,
is a cherry tree.

But, each year,
with the arrival of Spring,
she puts on
such a show of wild
colour
such a parade of extravagant
blossom,

I'm almost afraid
someone might see us together.

Realization

To be, for weeks, the glad
disciple of a single thought
has left me dazed
yet happy as a thrush.
It is the thought that
He, giver of the gifts we bring,
He who needs nothing
has need of us, and that
if you or I should cease to be,
He would die of sadness.

5
SCROLL

Hearing the River

It's true, only a fool or a madman
would claim to have broken open the final
scroll of meaning, and I am
not a fool, and not, I think, a madman.
But, early this morning, while working
at the more tiresome weeds in my small
garden, I think I stumbled on the mystery.
At one intake of breath I was no longer
myself, or I was myself, but I was now
strangely at one with all that is:
one with the earth, one with the sky and
the clouds, one with the weeds
and the stones and the tall grasses.
It was almost as if the hidden, lost language
of my soul was being revealed.
I found myself listening as never before.
And I was shocked. Not merely could I hear
a river of sound in the trees, I could
hear that same river flowing through my veins.

A Wound

What other name to call it? Beauty, when
it hits, pierces like a spear.

            That day I had gone
alone to the glen.
When, towards evening, the moment came
to turn back, I looked up
               and saw what seemed
like a vision:
the mountains, blood-red, and the clouds
above them, great
              scrolls of moving light.

I fell at once to my knees.

A Poor Man's Canticle

The ordinary knowledge of your love
is enough, Lord,
more than enough,
for those like me who have endured
the cold servitude of fear.

Now, like a tiny bird or wild
animal
imprisoned in its cage no longer,
I find I am released
into unexpected freedom.

Now
nothing pleases me more
than to stand head bare and foot bare
out in the wild
singing your praises.

Alive

These days I only half listen
to the messages from my weary bones.
   Hour to hour, with croaking voice,
they declare that my time is ending,
   that the play of sense is over.
But not one of the trials of old age,
   for all their grim authority,
can negate the nearness and beauty
   of the visible, tangible earth.
And there is no prophecy – no matter
   how dark – which can deny
the ordinary miracle of thoughts,
   dreams, passions, fears, all of them
alive to the end, all of them
   pulsing in the blood of my veins.

Brimming

Not light so much as darkness plays
on the path leading to the forest.
When, at length, I get to the place
and prepare myself for vigil,
the shadows will have deepened.
I will find a flat rock to sit on.
I will take a few deep breaths.
Then, wait, and then, wait further.
Next day, when I reach home,
I will find, perhaps, no words to say
except that all night long
the pond was brimming with rain.

A Practice Plain and Yet Extraordinary

As if it were possible to listen

to sunlight
or to feel the sound
of water

falling from the rocks above,

this is what I find
when I lift up my eyes

to contemplate
the Unseen,

when I hold out my hands

to grasp
the Impalpable.

This September

You have no need of visions,
no need of voices speaking
from the throat of the future.
Beyond the tufts of weed
and scrawny grass, now dry
with dust, now wet
with rain, from hour to hour,
from day to day, a hawthorn
reddens like a prophecy.

Your Lifespan

Do you
      want to know
            the true length of it?

The time it takes
         a swallow
             to dip
into a still pond
        and lift away.

In Extremis

Between
my body and my soul
an armistice
hangs by a thread.

I can still live. I can still
breathe.

My limbs
my arms and my legs
like sticks
glued to my body

and my heart's blood
chilled by fears
yet roused and giddy
with enchantment and remorse

still red
as a wild rowan berry!